THE PUZZLER'S GUIDE TO
OREGON

Games, Jokes, Fun Facts & Trivia
about the Beaver State

JEN FUNK WEBER

WEST
MARGIN
PRESS

For Barb, who notices everything.

ACKNOWLEDGMENTS

Thanks to puzzlers everywhere for being curious adventurers and brave souls willing to try, for untangling knots, and thinking critically. Thanks and cheers to the following people as well:

Jen, Olivia, and Rachel — for helping build the dream.

Turner Publishing — for keeping the dream alive.

Linda Stanek — for always lending her sharp eyes and brilliant brain.

Vicki Selvaggio and Storm Literary — for steady navigation, no matter the weather.

Beck — for still reading this.

Mike — for all those trips to Oregon.

Library of Congress Control Number: 2023942676

Hardcover 9781513141794
Paperback 9781513139272

Proudly distributed by Ingram Publisher Services

Published by Alaska Northwest Books®
an imprint of

WEST
MARGIN
PRESS

WestMarginPress.com

WEST MARGIN PRESS

Design by William Ruoto
Illustrations by Alexis Seabrook

HEY, PUZZLER!

Welcome to Oregon! Whether you're actually here in the state (will we see you?) or visiting through this book, we're excited to have you join us on this adventure.

CHIPPER
THE BEAVER

I'm Chipper. Building is my thing: lodges, dams, puzzles, you name it. Puzzles are all about looking at ideas from different angles, putting clues together, piece by piece, until you've got something that holds water. I'm also a fan of big and weird words. Grab some pencils and join us on this wacky tour of The Beaver State.

Puzzle tip: Don't fret if you can't solve a hard puzzle all at once. Chip away at it, maybe working from the middle or opposite end. You'll be surprised what you can accomplish taking a few small bites at a time.

I'm Queenie. Numbers and logic are what get my fins swishing. I think anything worth doing is worth overdoing, so look for some extra twists from me. I've never met a puzzle I couldn't complicate further.

Puzzle tip: Ever feel like you're swimming against the current of a puzzle? If you're fishing for some help, go over the instructions carefully to make sure you read them right the first time. Remember, some words have more than one meaning—and puzzles are designed to be tricky! Leap up those puzzle falls, y'all!

QUEENIE
THE CHINOOK

STUMPY
THE BOBCAT

Hey, humans, I'm Stumpy. I'm all about stealth and tracking. I like sneaky words with multiple meanings that lead you astray. And I like sniffing my way through mazes, especially tricky ones. I can race and pounce when I need to, but I prefer a leisurely pace, savoring details.

Puzzle tip: If you get hung up, slow down or stop. Walk away for a while, or take a cat nap. When you come back to the puzzle, you might see it differently.

Hi, people, I'm Spot. I like the view from aloft, where I can see the whole picture at once. From up here you can better see how pieces fit together to form a sometimes surprising whole. That's when things makes sense. I like mashing letters and words together so you have to sort them out to get the big picture.

Puzzle tip: When all else fails, you can find clues or the whole picture in the back of the book, as well as further explanations.

SPOT
THE OWL

TABLE OF CONTENTS

IN A NUTSHELL

This little fact highlights a big part of Oregon. Discover something important about the state by completing the writing on the wall. Place the 2x2 letter blocks in their proper places. Use the letters already on the wall as clues. Heads up: words are separated by black squares and wrap from one line to the next.

Y	O	U	■	C	A
N	■	R	E	A	D
■	T	H	E	■	W
R	I	T	I	N	G
■	O	N	■	T	H
E	■	W	A	L	L

N	E			L	Y	■
H	A		■			■
■	O	R	E	G		
	S	■			R	
	T	L			D	

O	F
O	N

A	R
L	F

F	O
A	N

■	I
E	S

 In a nutshell . . . is a tree waiting to grow! Oregon has 65 native tree species.

 Many are delicious! Some make excellent homes.

 I was using "nutshell" in the summary sense.

 Nutshells have a summertime connection?

 Oh, dear. It's going to be a long book.

1 THiNG 2 KNOW ABOUT OREGON

What gives this state its diverse range of terrain, temperature, plants, and animals is its different geographic regions. How many different regions does it have? To find out, figure out what number goes in the red circle below.

The three images represent three different numbers. The numbers at the end of the rows and columns are the sums of those images.

Oregon has _____ distinctly different geographic regions.

Why is it impossible to play hide-and-seek with a mountain?

They peak.

What did the beach say as the tide came in?

Long time no sea.

ONE-OF-A-KIND OREGON

All states have one, but Oregon's is unique.

Start at the ↓. Write every third letter on the spaces until you've used them all. If you do it right, you'll discover what Oregon has that no other state has.

S H G I A O D S R E A E D T G F W O L O N A

o _ _ _ _ _ _ _   _ _ _ _   _

_ _ _ _ - _ _ _ _ _ _   _ _ _ _ _ .

Vexillology (say vek-suh-LOL-uh-jee) is the study of flags, their history, symbolism, and useage.

Someone who studies flags is a vexillologist.

Someone who designs flags is a vexillographer.

A hobbyist who enjoys or collects flags is a vexillophile.

Chipper, you're vexing me.

AGATE HUNT

An agate is a kind of quartz rock with bands or clouds of different colors. Sometimes you can find them on the beach. Can you find the AGATE in the letters below? It appears only once in a horizontal, vertical, or diagonal line.

```
T  G  A  T  A  G  A  E  T  E
A  E  G  A  G  A  T  A  A  A
G  T  A  T  A  G  A  G  G  T
G  A  E  G  A  A  G  E  A  E
A  E  G  T  A  A  A  A  G  G
T  A  A  G  T  E  T  E  T  A
E  G  T  E  A  G  E  T  A  T
A  E  A  G  A  G  A  G  E  A
E  G  A  T  A  G  A  T  G  G
A  T  A  G  A  T  T  G  E  A
```

 Want to go agate hunting?

Of quartz you do!

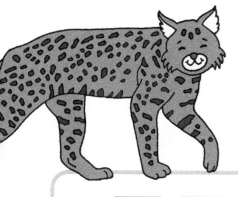

TANGLED TREES

Elevation, temperature, wind, rainfall, and soil conditions determine where different kinds of trees grow. Follow each tree's path, under and over crossing paths, to see where each grows.

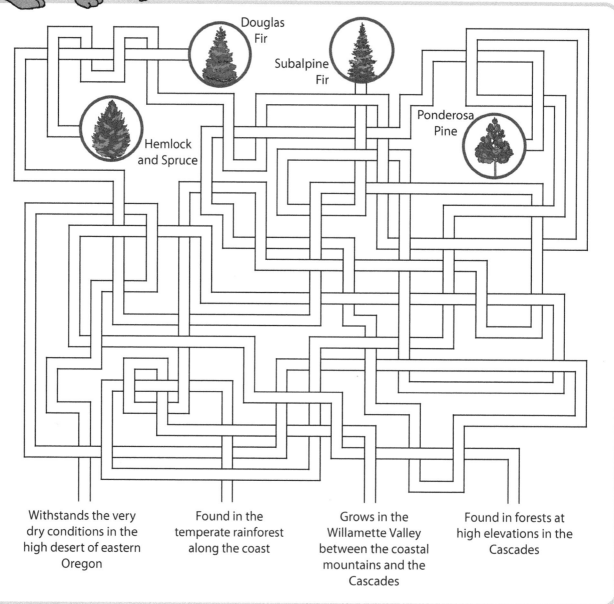

Douglas Fir

Subalpine Fir

Ponderosa Pine

Hemlock and Spruce

Withstands the very dry conditions in the high desert of eastern Oregon

Found in the temperate rainforest along the coast

Grows in the Willamette Valley between the coastal mountains and the Cascades

Found in forests at high elevations in the Cascades

Oregon leads the nation in producing softwood lumber and plywood.

Douglas fir is the most harvested tree in Oregon. It's the workhorse of the timber and building industries.

SWITCHAROO 1: NUTS ABOUT WORDS

Mature hazelnut trees typically produce 10 to 25 pounds of nuts a year.

Your instructions for these Switcharoo puzzles are to follow the instructions I give you. Get cracking!

Write HAZELNUT in the first box.

Reverse the two middle letters.

Change the first two letters to the ones that come after them in the alphabet.

Replace the 21st letter of the alphabet with the 18th letter, and eliminate the 26th letter altogether.

Remove all letters used in the word NOW.

Add the first letter in the word FRONT to the front of this word.

Reverse the third and fourth letters.

Most trees flower and pollinate in spring, but hazelnut trees flower and pollinate in winter.

Who eats nuts and bolts?

A squirrel in a hurry.

RANGE AND ____

Southeast Oregon is part of a larger region called "America's Great _____," and includes most of Nevada, half of Utah, and parts of California, Idaho, Wyoming, and Mexico. To find out what it is, place the five correct puzzle pieces in the rectangle. Watch out! Pieces might be rotated or flipped, and not all pieces are used. Write the letters of the correct pieces on the spaces. When you've got the right ones in, the word that fills the two blanks above will appear.

In this region, there are no outlets for any of the watersheds. That's easier to see from the air. That means all the water from rain and snow flows into lakes, is absorbed into the ground, or evaporates.

This enormous region is really a bunch of smaller, similar regions.

FROM THE BEGINNING

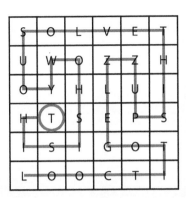

Complete the Rogue fact below by untangling the word string in the letters. I circled the first letter of the first word.

The string to the left untangles to say *This is how you solve this puzzle. Got it? Cool!*

Untangle the letters below and write them on the spaces.

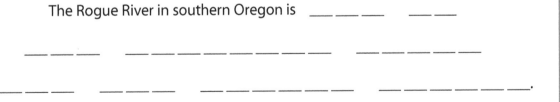

The Rogue River in southern Oregon is ___ ___ ___   ___ ___

___ ___ ___   ___ ___ ___ ___ ___ ___   ___ ___ ___

___ ___ ___ ___   ___ ___ ___ ___ ___   ___ ___ ___ ___ ___ ___.

 The Rogue River flows 215 miles from the Crater Lake area to the Pacific Ocean. Spot's fact refers to 84 miles of that.

 Did you know the beginning of the Rogue River is a spring?

 So the Rogue *springs* from the earth!

FIND 'EM WHERE THEY LIVE

Where will you most likely find these four Oregon birds?

Begin at the dot below each bird and follow the line downward. Every time you hit a horizontal line (one that goes across), you must take it. If you follow the lines correctly, you'll match each bird to its home territory. Write the birds' names below their habitats at the bottom.

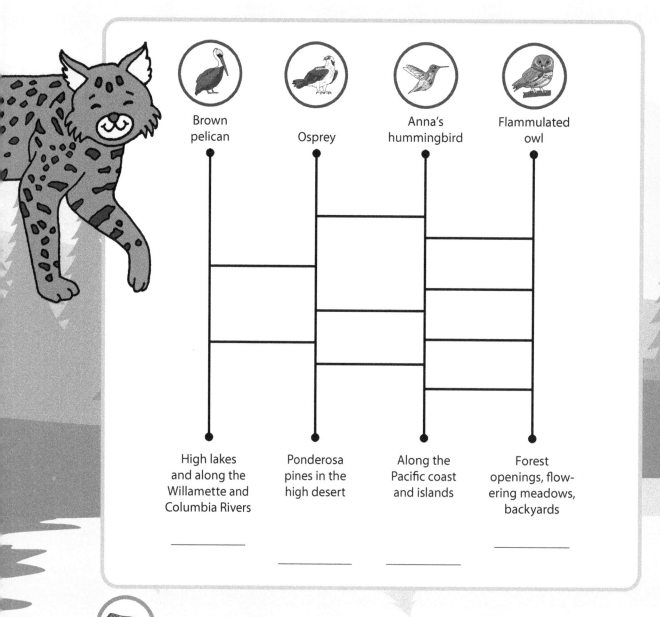

Brown pelican

Osprey

Anna's hummingbird

Flammulated owl

High lakes and along the Willamette and Columbia Rivers

_____

Ponderosa pines in the high desert

_____

Along the Pacific coast and islands

_____

Forest openings, flowering meadows, backyards

_____

 Flammulated? What a great word!

It means having flame-shaped markings.

 Get me a waterproof marker, and I'll be the first flammulated chinook!

14 FIND 'EM WHERE THEY LIVE

CAVE MARVEL

The National Park Service manages more than 3,900 cave systems. Oregon Caves is one of only three cave systems made of this.

Every word in Column B has the same letters as a word in Column A, plus one. Draw a line between word partners, then write the extra letter on the space provided. Unscramble the column of letters to reveal what the cave at Oregon Caves National Monument is made of.

Column A	Column B	Extra Letter
KARST	COMBINE	_____
ASSERT	MINERAL	_____
REMAIN	STREAK	_____
RIVER	PHRASES	_____
INCOME	ARRIVE	_____
SHAPES	STREAMS	_____

The cave at Oregon Caves National Monument is made of

____ ____ ____ ____ ____ ____.

Oregon Caves has at least eight endemic animal species, mostly tiny invertebrates. Endemic animals are ones that are not found anywhere else. They often develop by learning how to survive in unique environments—like caves.

Weird word alert! *Karst* is an area with lots of limestone, where underground streams have made ravines and caves. Good word for this puzzle, Queenie!

SHAKING THiNGS UP

Mt. Hood is a volcano and the tallest mountain in Oregon. It also has more of . . . well, it has more of *something* than any other volcano in the state.

To find out what that something is, write answers to the clues on the spaces, one letter on each space. Then tranfer the letters to the boxes with the same numbers.

A point of light in the night sky

___ ___ ___ ___
11   4   8   3

To move quickly back and forth or up and down; also an ending for milk___ and hand___

___ ___ ___ ___ ___
11   5   2   9   1

A closed shape with four straight sides the same length and four corners with the same angle

___ ___ ___ ___ ___ ___
11   6   7   2   3   10

Mt. Hood has more of these than any other volcano in Oregon:

1	2	3	4	5	6	7	8	9	10	11

Mt. Hood is 11,249 feet high.

It's a *stratovolcano.* Big word alert! That means it's a steep, conical volcano with layers (strata) of hardened lava, ash, and other volcanic material.

TIDEPOOL TENANTS

A tide pool is a body of sea water that remains as a rocky pool when the tide is low and the water moves back from the shore. Find these 13 things you might find in a tidepool. They might be forward, backward, up, down, or diagonal. The unused letters reveal two more things you can find in tide pools.

Oh, yeah. All the Es have been replaced with a 🌲. What can I say? I'm always hungry!

Hint: Circle individual letters instead of whole words to better isolate unused letters.

A	S	T	🌲	P	M	I	L	D	(B)
L	🌲	S	L	G	U	L	L	🌲	(A)
🌲	A	N	🌲	M	O	N	🌲	🌲	(R)
S	P	N	G	A	I	A	L	W	(C)
S	A	🌲	I	P	S	C	O	K	(T)
U	L	Y	L	H	A	T	S	C	(I)
M	M	U	T	N	C	🌲	A	O	(M)
R	C	C	R	A	T	R	C	R	(R)
S	🌲	A	L	🌲	T	T	U	C	(🌲)
H	B	🌲	L	I	A	N	S	R	(H)

ANEMONE
BARNACLE
GULL
~~HERMIT CRAB~~
LIMPET
MUSSEL
ROCKWEED
SCULPIN
SEA LETTUCE
SEA PALM
SEA STAR
SNAIL
URCHIN

Two more things you can find in tide pools:

__ __ __ __ __ and an __ __ __ __ __ __ __ __ __ __ __ __ .

Chipper, you've spelled "tide pool" as one word and two words. Which is it?

Good spotting, Spot! They're both right, and I couldn't make up my mind.

What did the fit tidepool say to the flabby tidepool?

Show me your mussels.

BACK WORD 1: FAMOUS FIGHTER

Some people actually come to Oregon to fight these. *Sheesh!*

The nine letters below make a word. Each letter is used once. The numbers and arrows tell you the order of the letters. For instance, the T in the center takes you one space up to an E, so in the word, E comes after T.

D is the last letter in the word. What letter has a number and arrow that takes you to the letter D? And what is the mystery word?

E
2→

E
2↓

A
1↓

S
1→

T
1↑

D
Last letter

H
2↑

E
1→

L
2←

This is a famous Oregon fighter:

								D

What did the fish mom tell her kids about eating worms?

Don't touch them; you'll get hooked.

ABOUT BURROWING OWLS

Burrowing owls often mate for life, and several pairs may nest in the same area.

Learn more as you find your way through this maze from START to FINISH. It will be easier if you correctly identify each statement as True or False.

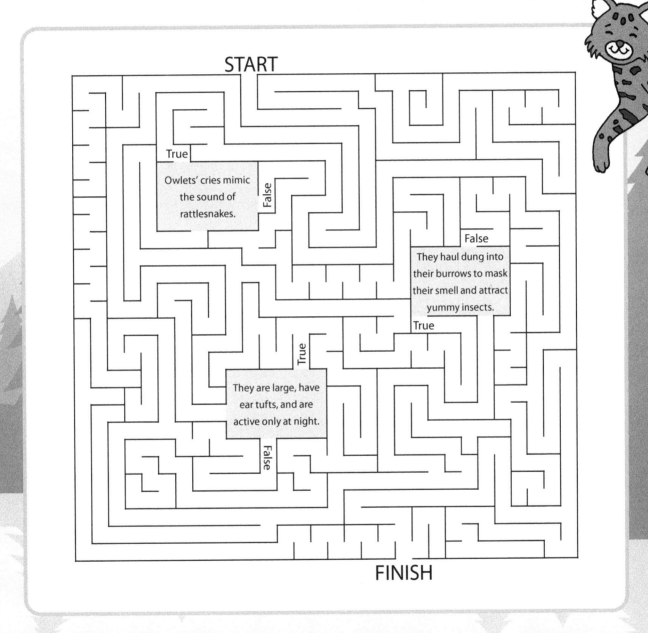

START

True

Owlets' cries mimic the sound of rattlesnakes.

False

False

They haul dung into their burrows to mask their smell and attract yummy insects.

True

True

They are large, have ear tufts, and are active only at night.

False

FINISH

Where are criminal owls sent?

Owlcatraz.

What are owls' favorite books?

Hoo-dunits.

VITAL VESSEL

It took months for emigrants to prepare for the journey from Missouri to the Pacific Coast over the Oregon Trail. What item was most important for many travelers?

To find out, place the Oregon Trail words in the crossword. Use the number of letters and intersecting letters to figure out where each word logically fits. I've done one to get you started. Transfer the numbered letters to the spaces with the same numbers. If you fill in the puzzle correctly, you'll reveal the answer to the question.

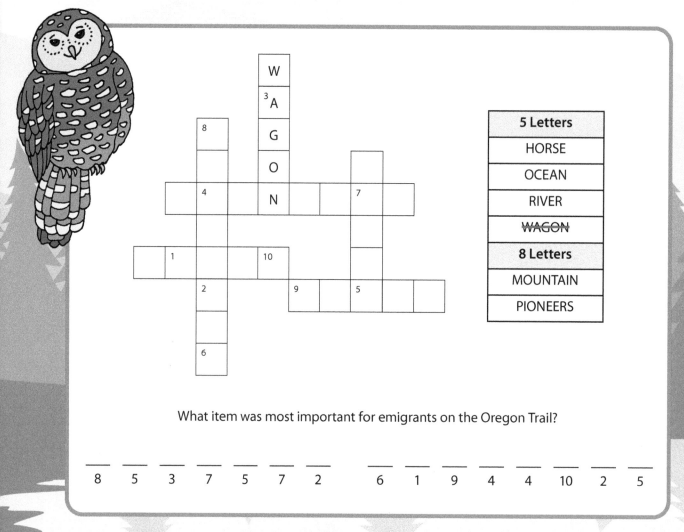

5 Letters
HORSE
OCEAN
RIVER
~~WAGON~~
8 Letters
MOUNTAIN
PIONEERS

What item was most important for emigrants on the Oregon Trail?

___ ___ ___ ___ ___ ___ ___   ___ ___ ___ ___ ___ ___ ___ ___
 8   5   3   7   5   7   2   6   1   9   4   4   10   2   5

That trip is way easier with wings!

Because there wasn't a single trail, but rather numerous paths, we call the length of the journey approximately 2,000 miles.

EXTREME OPPOSITES

Oregon is nicknamed The Beaver State. Beavers have been here a long, long time. Just how long? Solve the puzzle and see.

Complete the writing on the wall by placing the 2x2 letter blocks in their proper places. Use the letters already on the wall as clues. Heads up: words are separated by black squares and wrap from one line to the next.

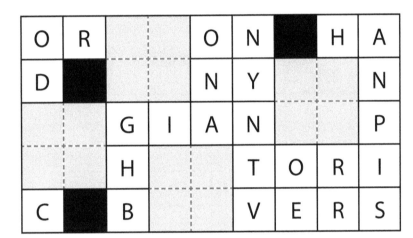

Beavers are the largest rodents in North America.

Our teeth continually grow. My teeth don't look unusually long because I wear them down chewing on trees, branches, and other plants.

What did Chipper charge the river with when it broke through his dam?

Illegal streaming.

1 THiNG 2 KNOW ABOUT LiGHTHOUSES

Oregon has over 360 miles of coastline. Dotted along that coastline are a number of lighthouses, helping ships navigate safely. How many lighthouses stand on the Oregon coast? To find out, figure out what number goes in the red circle below.

The three images represent three different numbers. The numbers at the end of the rows and columns are the sums of those images.

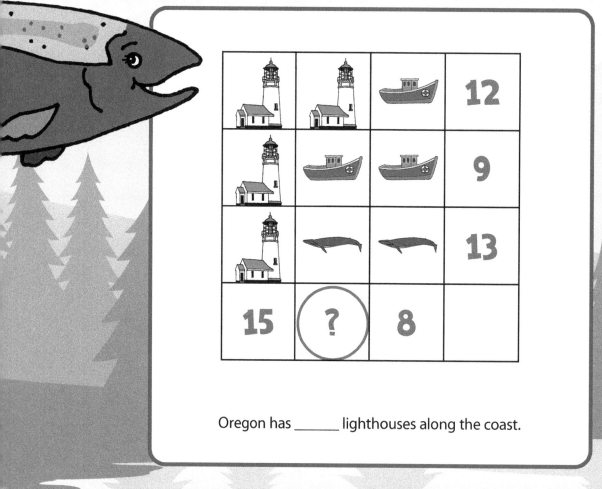

Oregon has _____ lighthouses along the coast.

The tallest Oregon lighthouse is Yaquina Head Lighthouse at 93 feet tall. The shortest is the Cape Meares Lighthouse at 38 feet tall.

Tillamook Rock Lighthouse, a.k.a. Terrible Tilly because it gets battered by waves, weather, and sea lions, briefly served as a *columbarium*. Big word alert! That's a place where cremated human remains are kept.

A CLAIM TO FAME

The geography and terrain around Hood River create perfect conditions for an activity that gives the town a special nickname.

Start at the ↓. Write every third letter on the spaces until all have been used. If you do it right, you'll be on close, personal terms with Hood River.

What's a nickname for Hood River?

W _ _ _ _ _ _ _ _ _ _   _ _ _ _ _ _ _

_ _   _ _ _   _ _ _ _ _ .

 Hood River is also known for its fruit.

 Over 15,000 acres around Hood River produce pears, apples, cherries, and grapes.

THE ELUSIVE COUGAR

Cougars are the largest wild cats in Oregon, and the second-largest in North America. They are mostly solitary and hunt between dusk and dawn, so they are rarely seen. Can you find the COUGAR in the letters below? It appears only once in a horizontal, vertical, or diagonal line. *Stick with it!*

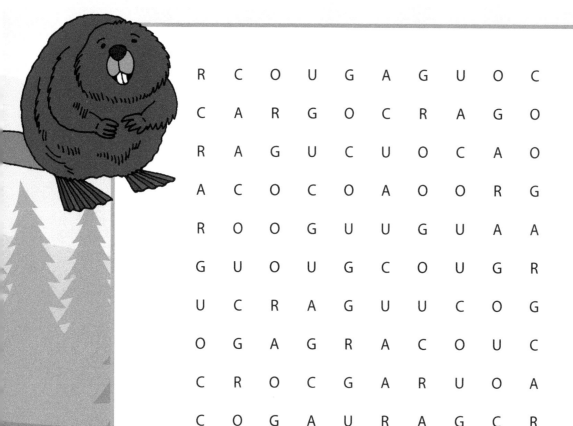

```
R  C  O  U  G  A  G  U  O  C
C  A  R  G  O  C  R  A  G  O
R  A  G  U  C  U  O  C  A  O
A  C  O  C  O  A  O  O  R  G
R  O  O  G  U  U  G  U  A  A
G  U  O  U  G  C  O  U  G  R
U  C  R  A  G  U  U  C  O  G
O  G  A  G  R  A  C  O  U  C
C  R  O  C  G  A  R  U  O  A
C  O  G  A  U  R  A  G  C  R
```

What's the difference between a photo of a cougar and a cougar that follows you?

One's a cat copy, the other's a copy cat.

Just because you don't see an animal doesn't mean it's not around. Look for animal signs: tracks and other markings, fur and bones, beds, places they've eaten, and poop. Everyone poops.

Mountain lion, panther, and puma are different names for the cougar.

Their primary food source is deer, but they will eat smaller mammals and birds too.

ANIMALS IN TROUBLE

Plants and animals in danger of becoming extinct are called *endangered*. Plants and animals at risk of becoming endangered are called *threatened*. Follow the paths of each plant and animal, under and over crossing paths, to see which are threatened or endangered.

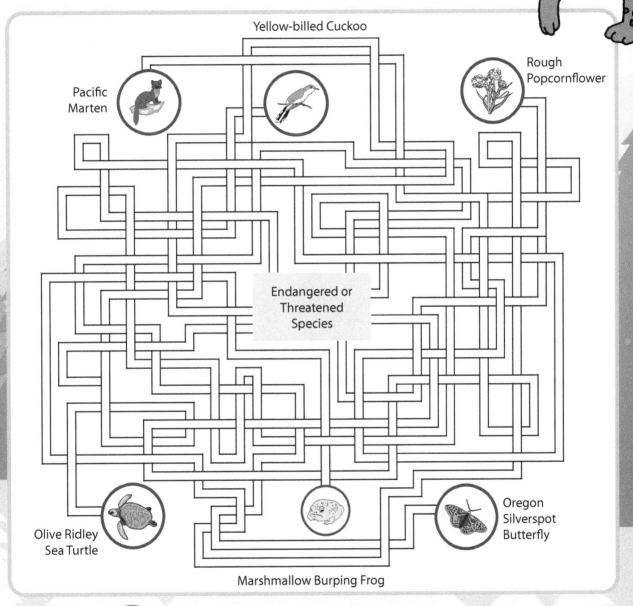

Yellow-billed Cuckoo

Pacific Marten

Rough Popcornflower

Endangered or Threatened Species

Olive Ridley Sea Turtle

Oregon Silverspot Butterfly

Marshmallow Burping Frog

Species disappear because of changes to the earth caused by nature or human activity.

We beavers were nearly wiped out due to over-trapping, but human awareness and management has restored our populations in many places.

SWITCHAROO 2: A SINKING FEELING

Oregon has 61 named volcanos.

Your instructions for these Switcharoo puzzles are to follow the instructions I give you. Get shaking!

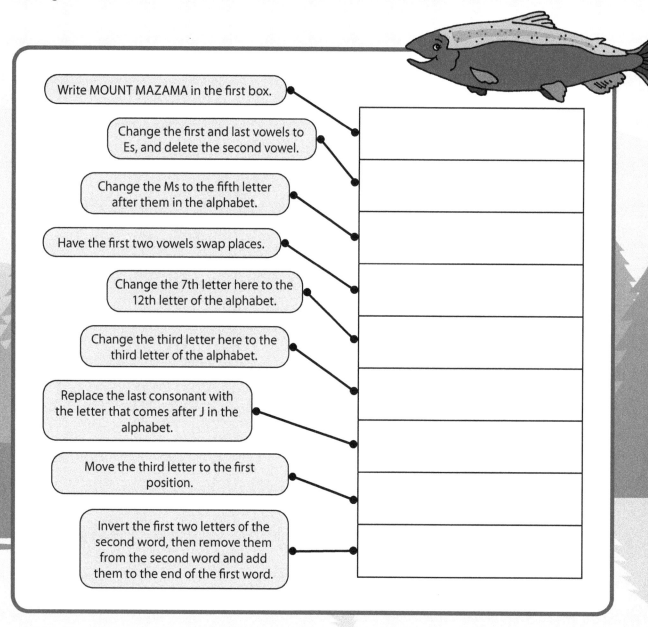

Write MOUNT MAZAMA in the first box.

Change the first and last vowels to Es, and delete the second vowel.

Change the Ms to the fifth letter after them in the alphabet.

Have the first two vowels swap places.

Change the 7th letter here to the 12th letter of the alphabet.

Change the third letter here to the third letter of the alphabet.

Replace the last consonant with the letter that comes after J in the alphabet.

Move the third letter to the first position.

Invert the first two letters of the second word, then remove them from the second word and add them to the end of the first word.

 90% of the continents and ocean basins are the result of volcanic activity.

 Earth is not the only place in the solar system that has volcanos. Jupiter's moon, Io, has the most volcanic activity in the solar system—that we know of, anyway.

. . . LIKE A FISH NEEDS A _____

Ever hear the joke about a person needing something like a fish needs a bicycle? It's funny because fish can't ride bicycles. However, fish really do use the tool in this puzzle.

To find out what it is, place the six correct puzzle pieces into the rectangle. Watch out! Pieces might be rotated or flipped, and not all pieces will be used. Write the letters of the correct pieces on the spaces. If you place them correctly, the name of this fish tool will appear.

I wouldn't mind having a bicycle. You'd pedal for me, right, Stumpy?

You bet!

BOOM AND BUST

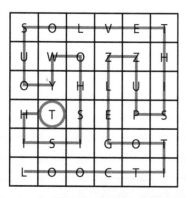

Oregon has over 200 ghost towns. Find out one reason why by untangling the word string in the letters. I circled the first letter of the first word.

The string to the left untangles to say *This is how you solve this puzzle. Got it? Cool!*

Untangle the letters below and write them on the spaces.

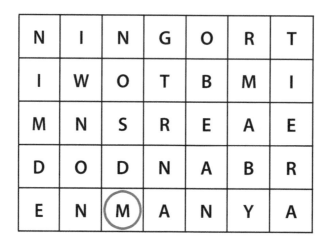

Why does Oregon have so many ghost towns?

— — — — —   — — — —

— — — — — — — — —   — — — — — —

— — —   — — — — — — —   — — — — — —.

What kind of horses do you find in ghost towns?

Night mares.

Where do you buy souvenirs in a ghost town?

A bootique.

That's a lot of ghost town jokes.

What do you call a ghost town full of cupcakes?

Desserted.

WHERE THE FUN IS

In Oregon, outdoor sports are *in*! Follow the lines to find out where you might go to get your sport on.

Begin at the dot below each sport and follow the line downward. Every time you hit a horizontal line (one that goes across), you must take it. If you follow the lines correctly, you'll match each sport to a place where it's done. Write the sports in the correct spaces at the bottom.

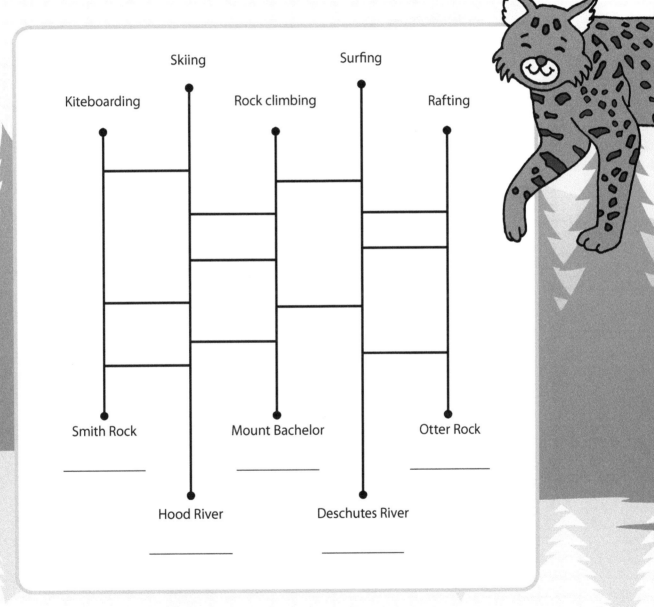

Skiing

Surfing

Kiteboarding

Rock climbing

Rafting

Smith Rock

_____

Mount Bachelor

_____

Otter Rock

_____

Hood River

_____

Deschutes River

_____

 What do you call a slow skier?

A slopepoke.

CARVING THE WAY

The Columbia River is one of just four rivers to carve a path through the Cascade Range to the Pacific Ocean. This Columbia River feature gets its name from a French word meaning throat or neck.

Every word in Column B has the same letters as a word in Column A, plus one. Draw a line between word partners, then write the extra letter on the space provided. Unscramble the column of letters to reveal this popular Columbia River feature.

Column A	Column B	Extra Letter
NEAR	GROWN	_____
POST	RANGE	_____
WORN	ALLOW	_____
PETS	SPORT	_____
WALL	STEEP	_____

This throat or neck feature is the Columbia River

____ ____ ____ ____ ____ .

The Columbia River is 1,243 miles long, the seventh longest river in the U.S.

The cascades, falls, and rapids made the Columbia River difficult and dangerous for Lewis and Clark's Corps of Discovery.

LIGHTHOUSE IDS

Every lighthouse has a unique flashing pattern so ships know where they are along the coast. What are these unique patterns called?

To find out, write answers to the clues on the spaces, one letter on each space. Then tranfer the letters to the boxes with the same numbers.

Water that leaks from clouds

___ ___ ___ ___
8   5   2   4

A sudden blast of wind

___ ___ ___ ___
3   7   1   6

The back part of a boat

___ ___ ___ ___ ___
1   6   9   8   4

Needing immediate attention

___ ___ ___ ___ ___ ___
7   8   3   9   4   6

A unique lighthouse flashing pattern is called a ____.

1	2	3	4	5	6	7	8	9

How do lighthouses communicate with boat captains?

Shine language.

MAKE IT MYRTLEWOOD

Oregon myrtle trees (*Umbellularia californica*) are ancient evergreens growing along the coast. Crafters make the 12 items below (and more!) from the pretty, fine-grained hardwood. Find those 12 myrtlewood items. They might be forward, backward, up, down, or diagonal. The unused letters spell another surprising item once made from myrtlewood in North Bend, Oregon.

Oh, yeah. All the Ts have been replaced with a . They were delicious!

Hint: Circle individual letters instead of whole words to better isolate unused letters.

```
S  V  A  S  E  B  M  R  Y  (N)
P  C  R  W  🌰 A  L  A  S  (I)
A  E  U  A  W  S  O  🌰 O  (G)
🌰 J  D  L  C  K  N  I  O  (H)
U  E  I  C  P  E  N  U  S  (🌰)
L  W  W  D  🌰 E  G  O  L  (L)
A  E  R  A  E  L  U  Y  E  (I)
G  L  N  L  A  L  S  R  M  (G)
O  R  N  A  L  W  O  B  E  (H)
O  Y  E  S  P  O  O  N  Y  (🌰)
```

BASKET
BOWL
GUITAR
JEWELRY
~~NIGHTLIGHT~~
ORNAMENTS
SALAD CLAWS
SCULPTURE
SPATULA
SPOON
TOYS
VASE

___ ___ ___ ___ ___ ___ ___ ___ ___   ___ ___ ___ ___

___ ___ ___ ___ ___ ___ ___ ___   ___ ___ ___ ___ ___ .

BACK WORD 2: FAMILY TIES

School kids elected the Western Meadowlark as the Oregon state bird in 1927.

The nine letters below make a word. Each letter is used once. The numbers and arrows tell you the order of the letters. For instance, the B in the center takes you one space down to an I, so in the word, I comes after B.

D is the last letter in the word. What letter has a number and arrow that takes you to the letter D? And what is the mystery word?

D
Last letter

B
1 →

L
2 ↓

K
1 →

B
1 ↓

C
2 ←

R
2 ↑

I
1 ←

A
1 ↑

Oregon's state songbird, the Western Meadowlark, is not a member of the lark family, no matter what its name suggests. It's a member of this family:

								D

Why do flies envy birds?
Because birds can fly, but flies can't bird.

The Western Meadowlark is also the state bird of Montana, Kansas, Nebraska, North Dakota, and Wyoming.

A FERNY THING HAPPENED ON THE WAY THROUGH THE FOREST

Oregon has many native ferns. Some are just a few inches high, others grow up to six feet tall. Stroll through this maze from START to FINISH, the way you'd stroll through a forest. It will be easier if you know whether the claims about ferns are True or False.

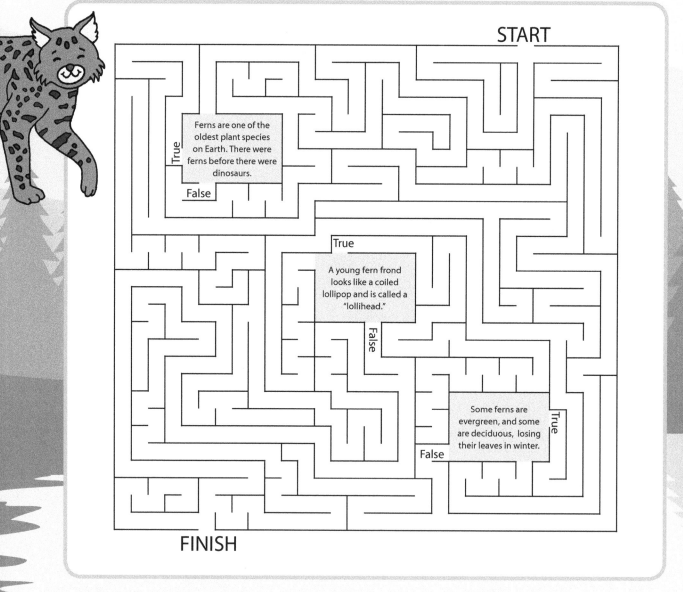

START

True

Ferns are one of the oldest plant species on Earth. There were ferns before there were dinosaurs.

False

True

A young fern frond looks like a coiled lollipop and is called a "lollihead."

False

Some ferns are evergreen, and some are deciduous, losing their leaves in winter.

True

False

FINISH

A house with pretty ferns in the garden beds is considered well *fernished*.

MADE iN MARiON

More than half the blackberries grown in Oregon are the Marion variety, a.k.a. Marionberries, named for Marion County where they were developed. Marionberries are a cross between what two blackberry varieties?

To find out, place the Marionberry words in the crossword. Use the number of letters and intersecting letters to figure out where each word logically fits. We've done one to get you started. Transfer the numbered letters to the spaces with the same numbers. If you fill in the puzzle correctly, you'll reveal the answer to the question.

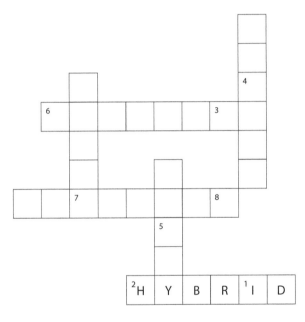

5 Letters
JELLY
JUICE
6 Letters
~~HYBRID~~
THORNY
8 Letters
CULTIVAR
ICE CREAM

Crossword entry: ²H Y B R ¹I D

What two blackberry varieties were crossed to make the Marionberry?

&

___ ___ ___ ___ ___ ___ ___   ___ ___ ___ ___ ___ ___ ___ ___
4   5   3   5   5   1   7   6   2   7   2   3   5   7   8

About 30 million pounds of Marionberries are produced in Oregon annually.

Big word alert! A cultivar is a variety of plant that has been bred for particular characteristics, like flavor, color, or lots of berries.

FOSSIL FINDS

The John Day Fossil Beds hold plant and mammal fossils from the Eocene epoch 45 million years ago to the Miocene epoch 5 million years ago. Unearth something exciting about the fossil beds.

Complete the writing on the wall by placing the 2x2 letter blocks in their proper places. Use the letters already on the wall as clues. Heads up: words are separated by black squares and wrap from one line to the next.

Y	O	U		C	A
N		R	E	A	D
	T	H	E		W
R	I	T	I	N	G
	O	N		T	H
E		W	A	L	L

A	L			O	U	G	
S	T			I	E	D	
O	R		O	V			1
0	0		Y	E		S	
		W		F	O	S	S	I
		A				S	T
I	L	L			U	N	D

E	R
A	R

T	H
U	D

R	E
F	O

H	
	F

N	E
L	S

 I'm going to look for dinosaur fossils!

 Want to hear a good fossil joke?

Give me a minute, and I'll dig one up.

 You won't find them here. This area was under the Pacific Ocean when dinosaurs were alive.

 The Eocene epoch started about 10 million years after dinosaurs became extinct. It was the Age of Mammals.

1 THiNG 2 KNOW ABOUT GOLD

The largest gold nugget found in Oregon came from Althouse Creek in southern Oregon in 1859. How much did it weigh? To find out, figure out what number goes in the red circle below.

The four pictures represent four different numbers. The numbers at the end of the rows and columns are the sums of those pictures.

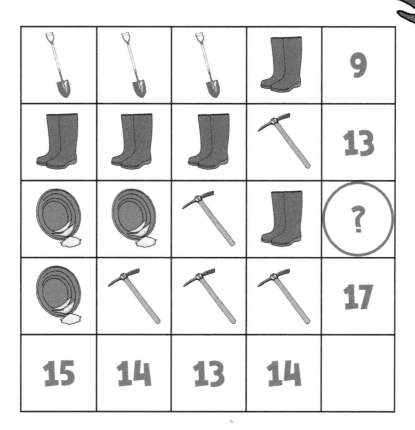

The largest gold nugget found in Oregon weighed _____ pounds.

I'll bet there's a bigger one out there somewhere!

Want to go look?

What is a prospector's favorite dessert?

Karat cake.

IN THEIR FOOTSTEPS

Newberry Volcano is the largest volcano in the Cascades Volcanic Arc, which stretches from southwestern Britsh Columbia to northern California. If you visit, you could walk in the footsteps of some famous people.

Start at the ↓. Write every third letter on the spaces until all have been used. If you do it right, you'll reveal some famous people who have been to the volcano.

What famous people visited the Newberry Volcano?

A _ _ _ _ _ _   _ _ _ _ _ _ _ _ _

_ _ _ _ _ _ _ _ _ _   _ _ _

_ _ _ _   _ _ _ _ _ _ _ _ _ .

Newberry Volcano is not a steep stratovolcano like Mt. Hood, Mt. Bachelor, or the Three Sisters. It's a shield volcano, so it's flatter and wider. The lava that flowed from Newberry was basalt, which is more fluid, so it was runnier and spread out before it hardened.

SAND DOLLAR SEARCH

Sand dollars are ocean animals. Sometimes, you can find their silver dollar-like endoskeletons (some might call them *shells*) on the beach. Can you find the SAND DOLLAR in the letters below? It appears only once in a horizontal, vertical, or diagonal line.

```
S  A  N  D  D  O  R  R  O  L
A  D  S  L  L  O  A  S  A  D
N  S  A  N  D  S  L  N  O  S
D  S  N  D  O  A  D  L  A  A
O  A  D  L  L  N  O  N  O  N
L  N  O  A  D  D  D  L  R  D
A  L  L  O  D  D  N  A  S  D
R  A  L  L  O  O  A  D  R  O
S  L  A  L  A  L  S  D  S  L
A  D  L  O  S  L  O  N  A  L
S  A  N  D  D  O  L  A  R  A
R  A  S  A  N  R  L  S  O  S
```

 Sand dollars are a kind of flat sea urchin. Their "shell" is the sand dollar's skeleton, and the proper name for it is "test."

 Other names for sand dollars are sand cake, cake urchin, and sea biscuit. In New Zealand, they're called sea cookies and snapper biscuits, and in South Africa, they're called pansy shells.

TIDE ZONES: WHO LIVES THERE?

The Low Tide Zone is only exposed during low tides, while the High Tide Zone is only under water during high tides. Follow the path from each tide zone, under and over crossing paths, to discover something that lives there.

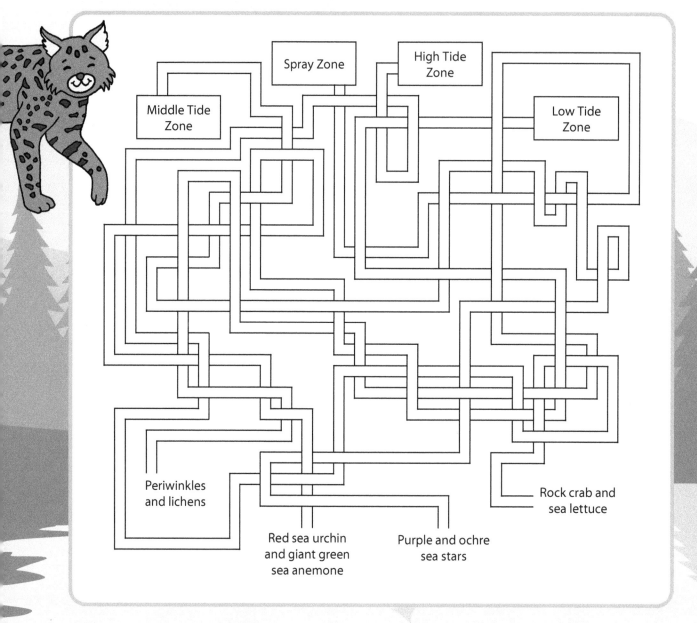

Spray Zone

High Tide Zone

Middle Tide Zone

Low Tide Zone

Periwinkles and lichens

Rock crab and sea lettuce

Red sea urchin and giant green sea anemone

Purple and ochre sea stars

What did the beach say as the tide came in?

Long time no sea.

SWITCHAROO 3: RODEO SLOGAN

The Pendleton Round-Up is over 100 years old. Follow the instructions to change PENDLETON to a familiar Round-Up slogan.

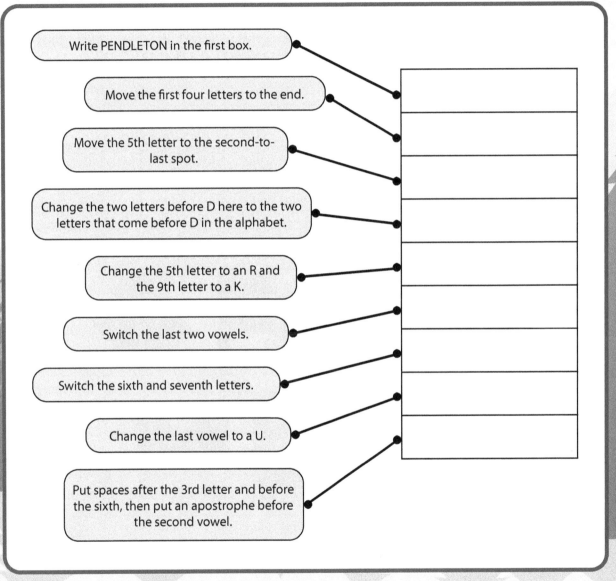

Write PENDLETON in the first box.

Move the first four letters to the end.

Move the 5th letter to the second-to-last spot.

Change the two letters before D here to the two letters that come before D in the alphabet.

Change the 5th letter to an R and the 9th letter to a K.

Switch the last two vowels.

Switch the sixth and seventh letters.

Change the last vowel to a U.

Put spaces after the 3rd letter and before the sixth, then put an apostrophe before the second vowel.

In 2013, the Happy Canyon show performed at the Round-Up was declared the official Outdoor Pageant and Wild West Show of Oregon.

A cowboy asked me to help round up 47 cows. I said, "Sure, pardner. That would be 50 cows."

What did the champion bull rider call his mounts?

My cattleacs.

A RIVER RUNS THROUGH IT

Hells Canyon is a 10-mile-wide canyon separating Oregon from Idaho. The maximum depth of the canyon is over 7,900 feet, making it the deepest in North America. What river carved this canyon?

To find out, place the five correct puzzle pieces in the rectangle. Watch out! Pieces might be rotated or flipped, and not all pieces are used. Write the letters of the correct pieces on the spaces. When you've got the right ones in, the name of this rock-carving river will appear.

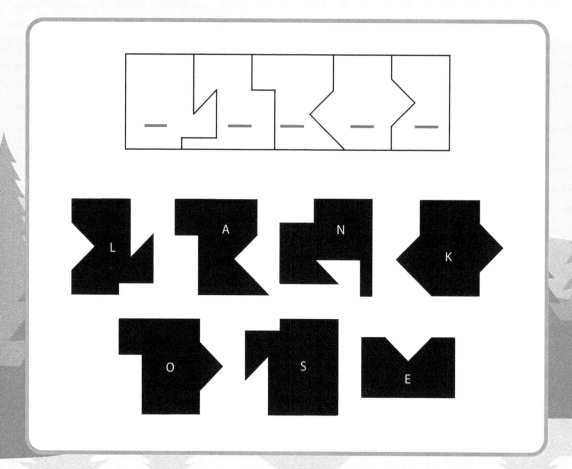

While there are a few roads into the canyon, hugging the steep walls, there are no roads across the canyon. The area is rugged.

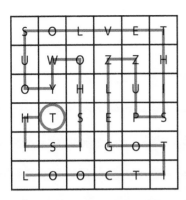

THE GRAY WHALE SCOOP

S	O	L	V	E	T
U	W	O	Z	Z	H
O	Y	H	L	U	I
H	(T)	S	E	P	S
I	S	S	G	O	T
L	O	O	C	T	

The most common whale off the Oregon coast is the gray whale. They have one way of feeding that no other whales use. Discover this unique technique by untangling the word string in the letters. I circled the first letter of the first word.

The string to the left untangles to say *This is how you solve this puzzle. Got it? Cool!*

Untangle the letters below and write them on the spaces.

U	D	F	R	O	M	T	H	E
M	(T)	I	N	A	L	L	A	O
P	H	M	O	U	T	S	M	C
O	E	A	N	I	A	R	T	E
O	Y	L	M	A	N	D	S	A
C	S	S	O	T	T	O	B	N

_____ _____ ____ ____

____ _____ _____

___ _____ ____

____ _____ .

How do you make a whale float?

Put it in a glass with ice cream and root beer.

To spot a whale, look for its spout: a puff of white blowing up from the ocean. When a whale surfaces, it exhales. When the warm, moist air from the whale's lungs meets the cool air above the ocean, it forms a column of mist.

NATIVE OR NOT?

Invasive plants and animals compete with native organisms for food and habitat, crowding out and threatening survival of native species. Which of these organisms are native?

Begin at the dot below each organism and follow the line downward. Every time you hit a horizontal line (one that goes across), you must take it. If you follow the lines correctly, you'll separate native from invasive. Write the plant and animal names in the correct boxes at the bottom.

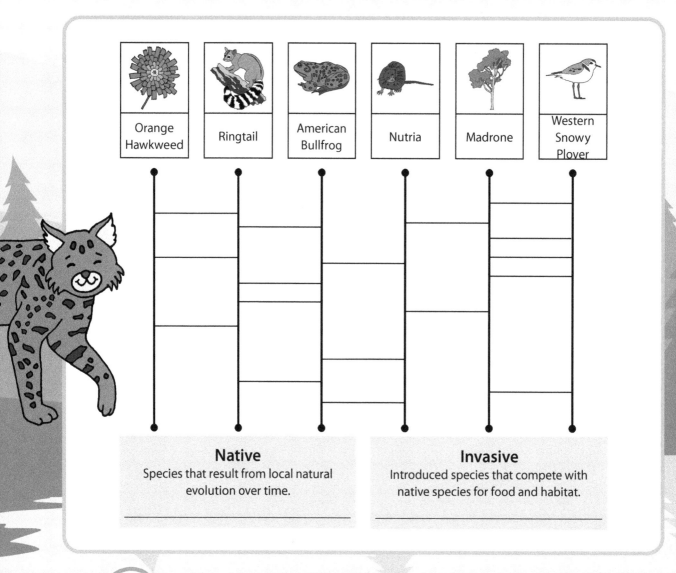

| Orange Hawkweed | Ringtail | American Bullfrog | Nutria | Madrone | Western Snowy Plover |

Native
Species that result from local natural evolution over time.

_____

Invasive
Introduced species that compete with native species for food and habitat.

_____

What do you call an invasive bird?

An illegal avian.

Weird word alert! *Avian* means of or related to birds.

ROCK STAR

Captain William Clark of the Lewis and Clark Expedition visited a particular rock in search of a dead blue whale. This rock has also starred in movies and novels. What is this rock?

Every word in Column B has the same letters as a word in Column A, plus one. Draw a line between word partners, then write the extra letter on the space provided. Unscramble the column of letters to reveal this rock star.

Column A	Column B	Extra Letter
NATURE	PIECRUST	_____
SEA LION	BASALT	_____
BLAST	TOENAILS	_____
TIDAL	UNEARTH	_____
PICTURE	ROTATE	_____
SHORE	DAYLIT	_____
OTTER	PROTECT	_____
POTTER	KOSHER	_____

Oregon's Rock Star is

__ __ __ __ __ __ __ __.

Those rock pillars and arches along the coast, surrounded by water, at least during high tide, are called sea stacks. Weather and waves have eroded all the material around them, leaving them isolated.

LARGEST FOUND IN THE U.S.—EVER!

What may have landed in Canada, was carried to the U.S., discovered in Oregon, and moved to New York?

To find out, write answers to the clues on the spaces, one letter on each space. Then tranfer the letters to the boxes with the same numbers.

2,000 pounds; used informally to mean *a lot*

$\overline{}_{1}\ \overline{}_{8}\ \overline{}_{5}$

It revolves around the earth and causes tides

$\overline{}_{3}\ \overline{}_{6}\ \overline{}_{2}\ \overline{}_{5}$

Ice flakes that fall from the sky to Earth

$\overline{}_{9}\ \overline{}_{5}\ \overline{}_{8}\ \overline{}_{7}$

Grown-up female human

$\overline{}_{7}\ \overline{}_{2}\ \overline{}_{3}\ \overline{}_{4}\ \overline{}_{5}$

What is this record-setting enormous thing?

1	2	3	4	5	6	7	8	9

What other records have been set in Oregon?

The most cartwheels in an hour: 1,714. That's 28.67 per minute.

According to Guinness World Records, we have the world's largest commercially available hamburger: 777 pounds.

The women's record for greatest distance on inline skates in 24 hours: 283.07 miles.

OREGON GROWN

Oregon has over 100 Farmers Markets where local fruits, vegetables, and more are sold. Find the fruits and vegetables in the letters. They might be forward, backward, up, down, or diagonal. The unused letters spell another very important thing grown in Oregon.

Oh, yeah. All the Es have been replaced with a 🌲. Making puzzles makes me hungry!

Hint: Circle individual letters instead of whole words to better isolate unused letters.

```
O  T  O  M  A  T  O  B  N  R
C  🌲 N  G  O  N  I  O  S  R
H  A  🌲 T  O  R  M  Y  P  🌲
🌲 P  C  K  L  M  A  S  R  W
R  G  T  O  I  D  U  🌲 C  O
R  🌲 A  S  S  W  R  N  P  L
Y  O  R  B  A  F  I  B  P  F
C  🌲 I  T  B  T  H  🌲 R  I
P  I  N  S  O  A  A  R  T  L
M  I  🌲 U  A  C  C  R  S  U
M  T  L  R  H  🌲 🌲 Y  S  A
🌲 P  U  O  L  A  T  N  A  C
```

BASIL
BOYSENBERRY
CABBAGE
CANTALOUPE
CAULIFLOWER
CHERRY
KIWI
MINT
NECTARINE
PEACH
PEAR
PERSIMMON
PLUOT
~~TOMATO~~

__ __ __ __ __ __ __   __ __   __   __ __ __ __

__ __ __ __ __ __ __ __ __

__ __ __ __ __ __ __ __   __ __ __ __ __ .

How do you fix a broken tomato?

With tomato paste.

How do you fix a broken pumpkin?

With a pumpkin patch.

BACK WORD 3: RABBIT RANGE

Pygmy rabbits live in, eat, and breathe this stuff.

The nine letters below make a word. Each letter is used once. The numbers and arrows tell you the order of the letters. For instance, the E in the center takes you one space down to a B, so in the word, B comes after E.

H is the last letter in the word. What letter has a number and arrow that takes you to the H? And what is the mystery word?

S 2→   G 1↓   A 1←

S 1↓   E 1↓   U 2←

H   B 1→   R 1↑
Last letter

Pygmy rabbits live in, eat, and breathe

								H

What's the difference between a gym rabbit and a clown rabbit?

One's a fit bunny, the other's a bit funny.

ABOUT AN OCTOPUS

Giant Pacific Octopuses live in the ocean off the Oregon coast. They are sometimes hauled to the surface clinging to crab pots. Discover more about them as you find your way through this maze from START to FINISH. It will be easier if you correctly identify each statement as True or False.

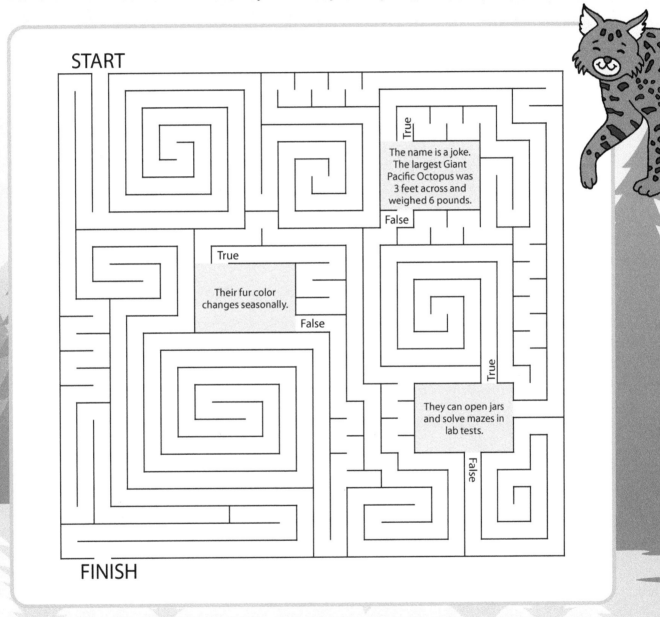

START

True

The name is a joke. The largest Giant Pacific Octopus was 3 feet across and weighed 6 pounds.

False

True

Their fur color changes seasonally.

False

True

They can open jars and solve mazes in lab tests.

False

FINISH

How do you make an octopus giggle?

With ten tickles (tentacles).

How do fish get to school?

They catch an octobus.

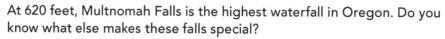

MULTNOMAH FALLS

At 620 feet, Multnomah Falls is the highest waterfall in Oregon. Do you know what else makes these falls special?

To find out, place the words in the crossword. Use the number of letters and intersecting letters to figure out where each word logically fits. We've done one to get you started. Transfer the numbered letters to the spaces with the same numbers. If you fill in the puzzle correctly, you'll reveal the answer to the question.

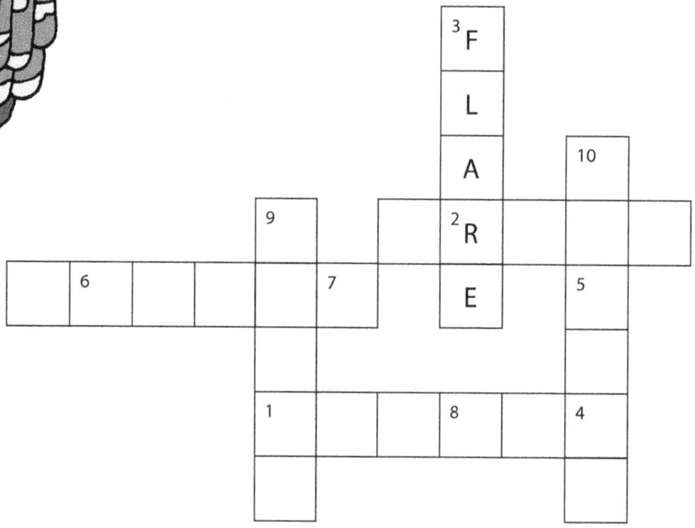

5 Letters
FLARE
PETAL
TRAIL
6 Letters
ALPINE
PLANET
WINTER

Crossword grid with numbered cells: 3F, L, A, 2R, E filled in vertically; numbered cells 10, 9, 6, 7, 5, 1, 8, 4.

Multnomah Falls is a

___ ___ ___ ___ ___ ___ ___ ___ ___
9   4   2   4   5   5   8   1   6

___ ___ ___ ___ ___ ___ ___ ___ ___
10 1   7   4   2   3   1   6   6

Some claim Multnomah Falls is the second-tallest year-round waterfall in the U.S., but that appears to be *falls advertising*.

What do you call a waterfall that's dried up?

A waterfell.

MOVE OVER, BLUE WHALE

Y	O	U		C	A
N		R	E	A	D
		T	H	E		W
R	I	T	I	N	G
		O	N		T	H
E		W	A	L	L

In the Malheur National Forest in the Blue Mountains of eastern Oregon, something has disturbed what was once considered the blue whale's place in the world.

To find out what it is, complete the writing on the wall by placing the 2x2 letter blocks in their proper places. Use the letters already on the wall as clues. Heads up: words are separated by black squares and wrap from one line to the next.

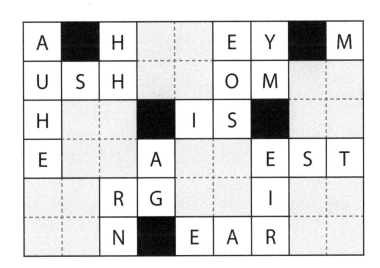

Move over, Blue Whale, there's not *mushroom* here!

The Malheur National Forest also contains high desert grasslands, juniper and sage, pine, fir, and other trees.

1 THiNG 2 KNOW ABOUT WEiRD PORTLAND

Guinness World Records named a park in Portland the Smallest Park in the World. What is the diameter of this circular park? To find out, figure out what number goes in the red circle below.

The three images represent three different numbers. The numbers at the end of the rows and columns are the sums of those images.

The World's Smallest Park in Portland, Oregon is _____ inches in diameter.

 Oregon has just one National Park (Crater Lake), but it has 111 State Parks.

 And Portland has 154 developed parks.

 The largest Portland park is Forest Park with 5,172.14 acres.

 Why won't you see mummies in a Portland park?

They're afraid that if they relax, they'll unwind.

PEST CONTROL

Oregon has 15 species of bats, eight of which have small or declining populations or are considered "at risk."

Start at the ↓. Write every third letter on the spaces until all have been used. If you do it right, you'll reveal one reason we should love bats.

(circle of letters, reading clockwise from the arrow: R E T A C H B T O A S U T I S C N A A N N D E H I A O N T U S A)

What is one reason we should love bats?

A ___ ___ ___

_ _____ _____

__ ___ _____.

Bats are the only flying mammal. Flying squirrels don't really fly. They glide.

Bats are pollinators, like bees and butterflies. Hundreds of plant species depend on them.

ROCKHOUND

Thundereggs are hollow rocks filled with mineral deposits. People slice them to reveal cool patterns and colors. Can you find the THUNDEREGG in the letters below? It appears only once in a horizontal, vertical, or diagonal line. Rock on!

```
T  R  T  H  U  N  D  E  R  T  U  T
G  H  H  U  G  G  E  R  H  U  H  G
T  H  U  N  D  E  R  E  G  N  U  E
G  D  N  N  U  H  E  U  N  N  G  G
E  N  D  T  G  D  T  D  G  D  G  R
R  G  E  G  N  E  R  D  E  E  E  E
E  U  R  U  T  G  R  N  R  R  R  D
D  T  H  U  N  D  E  R  E  G  G  N
N  T  E  D  N  U  H  T  D  G  U  U
U  G  G  T  G  E  R  E  N  E  G  H
H  E  D  G  E  R  E  D  N  U  H  T
T  H  U  N  D  E  R  R  E  G  G  U
```

I just figured out why playing "catch" with rocks is a bad idea.

It just hit you, eh?

Thundereggs are so pretty!

Yeah.

MASCOT LOVE

Oregon's got some crazy-cool sports mascots. Follow the path of each mascot, under and over crossing paths, to discover which teams these mascots support.

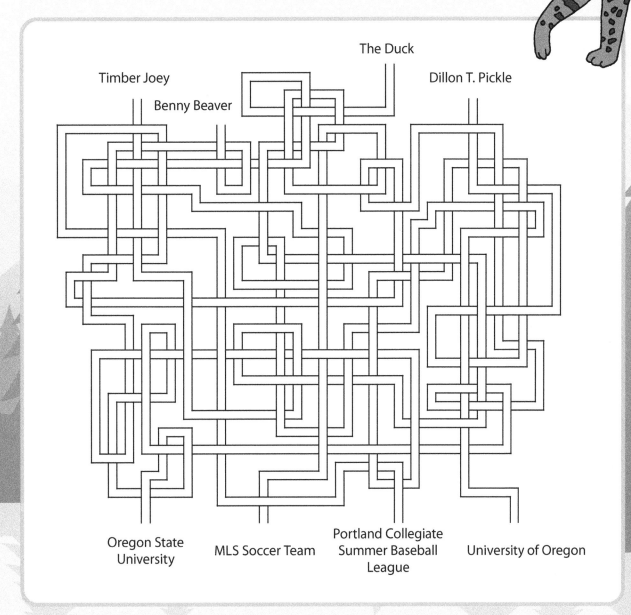

Timber Joey

Benny Beaver

The Duck

Dillon T. Pickle

Oregon State University

MLS Soccer Team

Portland Collegiate Summer Baseball League

University of Oregon

 I like the rainbow trout mascot at South Wasco County High School. The teams are called the "redsides."

 Some other high school mascots are the Locomotives, Loggers, Prospectors, and Cheesemakers.

SWITCHAROO 4: PLANT A PEAR TREE

The pear is Oregon's official state fruit, so let's plant a pear tree. Your instructions for Switcharoo puzzles are to follow the instructions I give you below. Heads up! We start at the bottom this time because, you know, trees grow *up*.

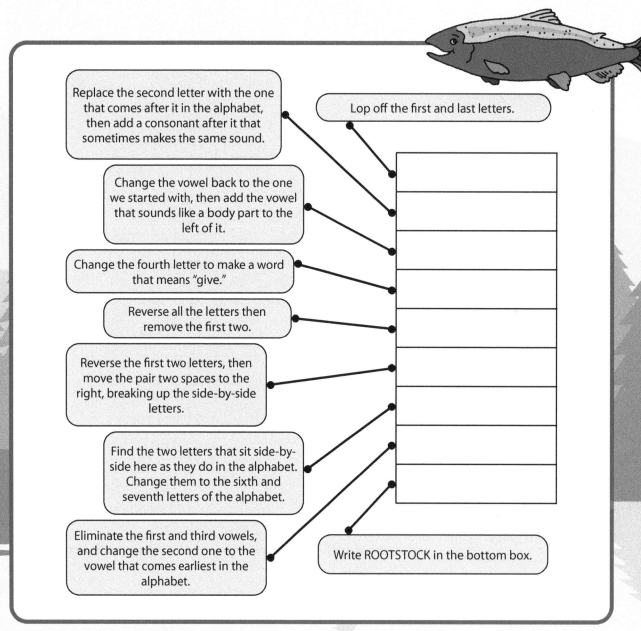

Replace the second letter with the one that comes after it in the alphabet, then add a consonant after it that sometimes makes the same sound.

Lop off the first and last letters.

Change the vowel back to the one we started with, then add the vowel that sounds like a body part to the left of it.

Change the fourth letter to make a word that means "give."

Reverse all the letters then remove the first two.

Reverse the first two letters, then move the pair two spaces to the right, breaking up the side-by-side letters.

Find the two letters that sit side-by-side here as they do in the alphabet. Change them to the sixth and seventh letters of the alphabet.

Eliminate the first and third vowels, and change the second one to the vowel that comes earliest in the alphabet.

Write ROOTSTOCK in the bottom box.

Pear tree wood is used to make furniture, instruments, and more.

Pears are picked when they're mature, but not quite ripe. They ripen off the tree.

ON THE NOSE

The genus of this official state animal, and its relatives, is Oncorhynchus (say ON-cor-ING-kus), which means *hooked nose*.

Identify this animal by placing the six correct puzzle pieces into the rectangle. Watch out! Pieces might be rotated or flipped, and not all pieces are used. Write the letters of the correct pieces on the spaces. If you place them correctly, you'll get this answer on the nose.

 If they don't like their hooked noses, they can get new ones at the ol' factory.

 I'm built upside down: my feet smell and my nose runs.

 What comes out of a pig's nose?

Hamboogers.

COLOR ME CURIOUS

S	O	L	V	E	T
U	W	O	Z	Z	H
O	Y	H	L	U	I
H	(T)	S	E	P	S
I	S	I	G	O	T
L	O	O	C	T	

Have you ever noticed that something is missing from the rainbow of roses? Discover what is missing and why by untangling the word string in the letters. I circled the first letter of the first word.

The string to the left untangles to say *This is how you solve this puzzle. Got it? Cool!*

Untangle the letters below and write them on the spaces.

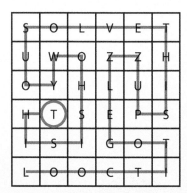

S	L	B	D	N	A	(R)	C	K
R	A	B	L	U	E	O	A	A
O	C	E	U	R	T	S	L	G
L	K	A	K	E	S	E	S	E
O	C	M	T	A	H	T	E	N

_ _ _ _ _ _ _   _ _ _ _ _   _ _   _ _ _ _ _   _ _ _ _ _

_ _ _ _ _ _   _ _ _ _ _ - _ _ _ _

_ _ _ _ _ _   _ _ _ _ _ _ _ _.

Rose petals are edible. They're used to make tea, jelly, and syrup. Rose water (water that has had rose petals soaked in it) flavors Persian, Indian, and Chinese dishes.

Roses produce an edible fruit called a rose hip that is loaded with Vitamin C.

The rose became the official flower of the United States in 1986.

THE LAY OF THE LANDMARKS

Where in Oregon would you go to see these cool sights?

Begin at the dot below each landmark and follow the line downward. Every time you hit a horizontal line (one that goes across), you must take it. If you follow the lines correctly, you'll match each landmark to where it's located. Write the landmarks in the correct spaces at the bottom.

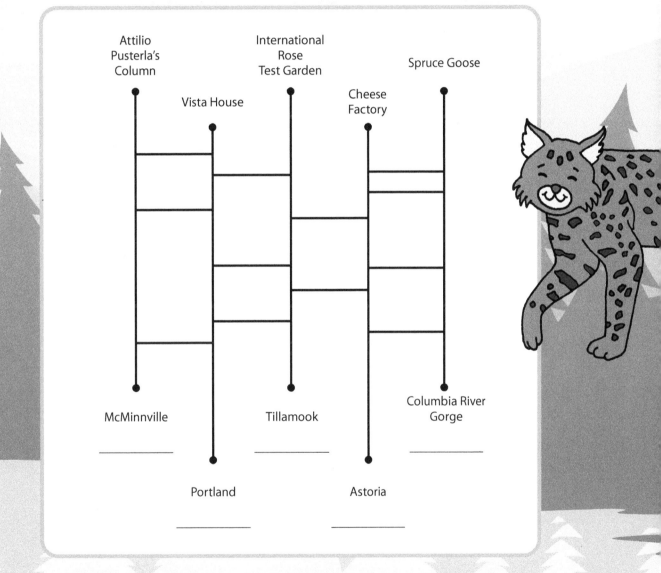

There is soooo much to see here in Oregon! What about the Oregon Dunes, Bonneville Dam, Silver Falls?

Few of us can cover as much ground as you do, Spot.

BEACH TREASURES

Oregon's beaches are known for their shell, agate, and jasper treasures. Do you know what else you can find during low tides?

Every word in Column B has the same letters as a word in Column A, plus one. Draw a line between word partners, then write the extra letter on the space provided. Unscramble the column of letters to reveal another beach treasure.

Column A	Column B	Extra Letter
MARGINS	PROCESS	_____
SECRET	PETRIFY	_____
BURIED	RECITES	_____
CORPSE	ORGANISM	_____
REACH	REBUILD	_____
PYRITE	SEMINARS	_____
REMAINS	SEARCH	_____

You might find these on Oregon's beaches:

—— —— —— —— —— —— ——.

Why don't oysters share their pearls?

They're shellfish.

What do you call a beach where the sand has washed away?

A shore loser.

NATURE'S BONSAI

They might look funny and misshapen, but their ability to survive is impressive. Look for these on coastal cliffs where strong winds blow.

To find out what you're looking for, write answers to the clues on the spaces, one letter on each space. Then tranfer the letters to the boxes with the same numbers.

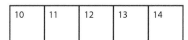

Look for, or Hide and ___

$\overline{14}\ \overline{13}\ \overline{12}\ \overline{1}$

Nil, naught, nothing

$\overline{9}\ \overline{13}\ \overline{2}\ \overline{7}$

Severe weather with wind, rain, snow, thunder, or lightning

$\overline{14}\ \overline{10}\ \overline{7}\ \overline{11}\ \overline{5}$

A sense of ___ allows someone to think something is funny

$\overline{6}\ \overline{3}\ \overline{4}\ \overline{7}\ \overline{2}$

The land beside an ocean, lake, or river

$\overline{14}\ \overline{6}\ \overline{7}\ \overline{11}\ \overline{12}$

The sound leaves make on a windy day

$\overline{2}\ \overline{3}\ \overline{14}\ \overline{10}\ \overline{8}\ \overline{13}$

1	2	3	4	5	6	7	8	9

10	11	12	13	14

A bunch of these guys live in my old-growth forest neighborhood.

Why was the kid afraid of the forest?

It looked shady.

STATE SYMBOLS

Find these 13 state symbols. They might be forward, backward, up, down, or diagonal. The unused letters reveal two more symbols.

Oh, yeah. All the Es have been replaced with a . You know why.

Hint: Circle individual letters instead of whole words to better isolate unused letters.

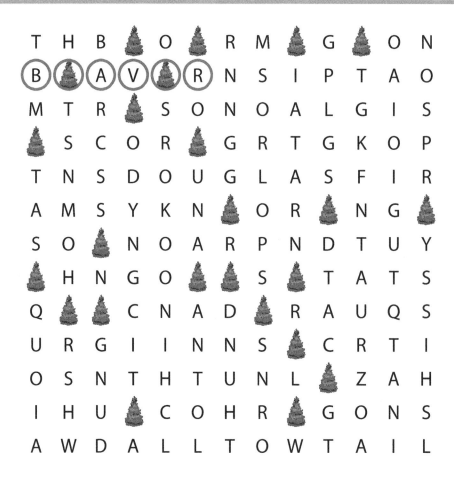

```
T  H  B  🌲 O  🌲 R  M  🌲 G  🌲 O  N
B  🌲 A  V  🌲 R  N  S  I  P  T  A  O
M  T  R  🌲 S  O  N  O  A  L  G  I  S
🌲 S  C  O  R  🌲 G  R  T  G  K  O  P
T  N  S  D  O  U  G  L  A  S  F  I  R
A  M  S  Y  K  N  🌲 O  R  🌲 N  G  🌲
S  O  🌲 N  O  A  R  P  N  D  T  U  Y
🌲 H  N  G  O  🌲 🌲 S  🌲 T  A  T  S
Q  🌲 🌲 C  N  A  D  🌲 R  A  U  Q  S
U  R  G  I  I  N  N  S  🌲 C  R  T  I
O  S  N  T  H  T  U  N  L  🌲 Z  A  H
I  H  U  🌲 C  O  H  R  🌲 G  O  N  S
A  W  D  A  L  L  T  O  W  T  A  I  L
```

(BEAVER circled)

More Oregon numbers: It is the 33rd state, admitted to the Union in 1859.

Why were Always-Late Leyla, Sloppy Poppy, and Mixed-Up Merlin sent to Oregon?

To get Oregonized.

Animal:
BEAVER

Nut:
HAZELNUT

Flower:
OREGON GRAPE

Dance:
SQUARE DANCE

Fish:
CHINOOK

Fossil:
METASEQUOIA

Raptor:
OSPREY

Gemstone:
SUNSTONE

Tree:
DOUGLAS FIR

Beverage:
MILK

Fruit:
PEAR

Rock:
THUNDEREGG

Crustacean:
DUNGENESS CRAB

___ ___ ___   ___ ___ ___ ___ ___   ___ ___ ___ ___ ___   ___ ___ ___ ___

___ ___   ___ ___ ___ ___ ___ ___ ,   ___ ___ ___   ___ ___ ___ ___ ___ ___ ___ ,

___ ___ ___   ___ ___ ___   ___ ___ ___ ___ ___   ___ ___ ___ ___ ___ ___   ___ ___

___ ___ ___   ___ ___ ___ ___ ___ ___   ___ ___ ___ ___ ___ ___ ___ ___ ___ ___ .

In 2017, the Oregon legislature changed the State Bird designation: the Western Meadowlark became the state songbird and the Osprey became the state raptor.

BACK WORD 4: A BURROWER?

There's plenty to explore in Oregon if you're one of these.

The 12 letters below make a word. Each letter is used once. The numbers and arrows tell you the order of the letters. For instance, the I in the top left corner takes you three spaces right to an S, so in the word, S comes after I.

T is the last letter in the word. What letter has a number and arrow that takes you to the letter T? And what is the mystery word?

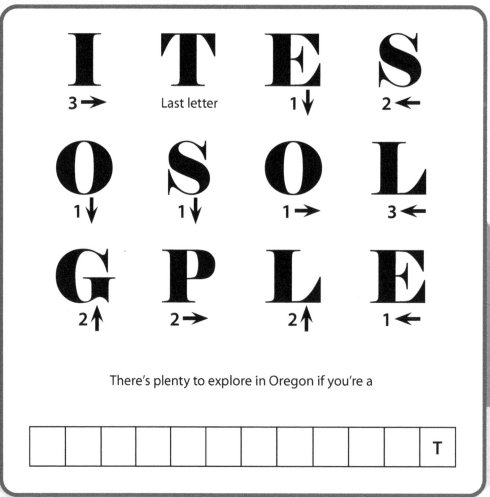

I	T	E	S
3 →	Last letter	1 ↓	2 ←
O	S	O	L
1 ↓	1 ↓	1 →	3 ←
G	P	L	E
2 ↑	2 →	2 ↑	1 ←

There's plenty to explore in Oregon if you're a

											T

Oregon is home to many burrowers: pocket gophers, shrews, moles, snakes, ants, rabbits, river otters, burrowing owls, and more.

Some beavers burrow into riverbanks instead of building dams and lodges.

FRUIT LOOP

No need to be in Hood River to enjoy this Fruit Loop. Make your way from START to FINISH collecting all the fruit in the loop.

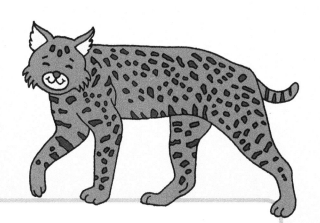

START **FINISH**

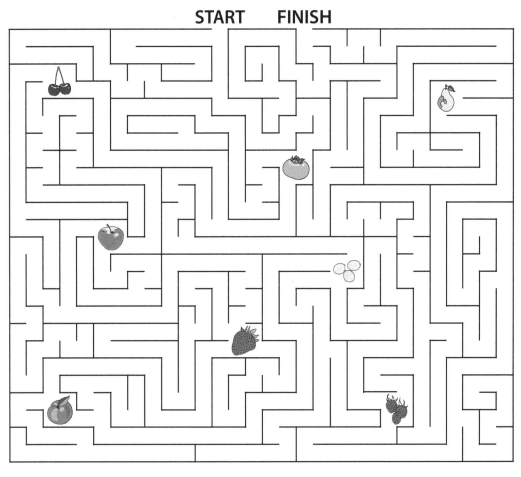

 The Fruit Loop in Hood River is a 35 mile scenic drive through family farms, orchards, vineyards, and more.

 On the loop, you can pick fruit and flowers; discover art and crafts; sample baked goods, ice cream, and cider; explore farms and gardens.

HiDDEN iN PLAiN SiGHT

Until 2017, Humboldt's Flying Squirrels were thought to be Northern Flying Squirrels. That was a mistake. They are a whole different species. What do you call an animal that looks like another but is, in fact, different?

To find out, place the words in the crossword. Use the number of letters and intersecting letters to figure out where each word logically fits. We've done one to get you started. Transfer the numbered letters to the spaces with the same numbers. If you fill in the puzzle correctly, you'll reveal the answer to the question.

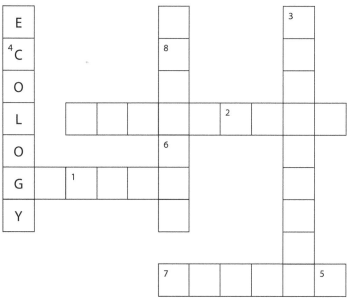

| 6 Letters |
| GLIDER |
| SECRET |
| 7 Letters |
| ~~ECOLOGY~~ |
| MYSTERY |
| 9 Letters |
| NOCTURNAL |
| PARACHUTE |

Humboldt's Flying Squirrels are a

___ ___ ___ ___ ___ ___ ___   ___ ___ ___ ___ ___ ___ ___ .
 4   2   8   3   5   1   4   7   3   6   4   1   6   7

Flying squirrels have a furry, parachute-like flap of skin between their front and back limbs that catches air as they fall, allowing them to glide from branch to branch and tree to tree.

They huddle together for warmth, and flying squirrels are known to share their nests with bats and other animals.

ANSWERS

IN A NUTSHELL

N	E	A	R	L	Y	
H	A	L	F		O	F
	O	R	E	G	O	N
	I	S			F	O	R
E	S	T	L	A	N	D

1 THING 2 KNOW ABOUT OREGON

 = 1   = 2   = 3

Oregon has 6 wildly different geographic regions.

Oregon can be divided into these 6 regions:

1. Coast range (rainforest)
2. Willamette lowland (farmland)
3. Cascade mountains (volcanoes)
4. Klamath mountains (coniferous forests)
5. Columbia River Plateau
6. Basin and Range region (high desert)

The variations in these regions allow a wide variety of trees to grow. Note the changes in the terrain and trees as you move around the state. The differences are stark and beautiful.

ONE-OF-A-KIND OREGON

OREGON HAS A TWO-SIDED FLAG.

AGATE HUNT

```
T G A T A G A E T E
A E G A G A T A A A
G T A T A G A G G T
G A E G A A G E A E
A E G T A A A A G G
T A A G T E T E T A
E G T E A G E T A T
A E A G A G A G E A
E G A T A G A T G G
A T A G A T T G E A
```

TANGLED TREES

Hemlock and Spruce – Found in the temperate rainforest along the coast

Douglas fir – Grows in the Willamette Valley between the coastal mountains and the Cascades

Subalpine fir – Found in forests at high elevations in the Cascades

Ponderosa pine – Withstands the very dry conditions in the high desert of eastern Oregon

SWITCHAROO 1: NUTS ABOUT WORDS

HAZELNUT - HAZLENUT - IBZLENUT - IBLENRT - IBLERT - FIBLERT - FILBERT

I get it! *Hazelnuts* are also called *filberts*.

RANGE AND _____

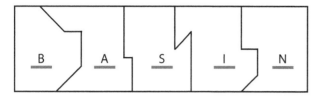

Southeast Oregon is part of America's Great BASIN.

Southeast Oregon's Basin and Range ecoregion is part of the larger Great Basin. This area includes several flat basins separated by isolated mountains (a.k.a. ranges). It's the dry, high desert part of the state.

FROM THE BEGINNING

	G	I	R	O	E	H	T
N	A	L	O	N	E	O	F
E	C	E	I	G	H	T	W
N	S	D	N	A	D	L	I
I	C	R	I	V	E	R	S

The Rogue River in southern Oregon is ONE OF THE ORIGINAL EIGHT WILD AND SCENIC RIVERS.

In 1968, Congress passed the Wild and Scenic Rivers Act to protect eight US rivers for their important wild, scenic, and/or recreational features.

FIND 'EM WHERE THEY LIVE

Brown pelican - Along the Pacific coast and islands

Osprey - High lakes and along the Willamette and Columbia Rivers

Anna's hummingbird - Forest openings, flowering meadows, backyards

Flammulated owl - Ponderosa pines in the high desert

CAVE MARVEL

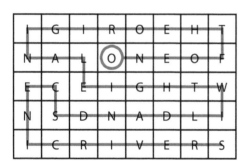

Column A		Column B	Extra Letter
KARST		COMBINE	B
ASSERT		MINERAL	L
REMAIN		STREAK	E
RIVER		PHRASES	R
INCOME		ARRIVE	A
SHAPES		STREAMS	M

The cave at Oregon Caves National Monument is made of MARBLE.

SHAKING THINGS UP

STAR

SHAKE

SQUARE

Mt. Hood has more EARTHQUAKES than any other volcano in Oregon.

TIDEPOOL TENANTS

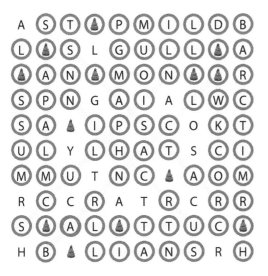

Unused letters: Two more things you can find in tidepools: ALGAE and an OYSTERCATCHER.

BACK WORD 1: FAMOUS FIGHTER

This is a famous Oregon fighter: STEELHEAD

Steelhead are sometimes called steelhead trout. They are the same genus as salmon, and, like Queenie, are anadromous (say uh-NAD-ruh-muss). That means they spend part of their lives in freshwater and part at sea.

ABOUT BURROWING OWLS

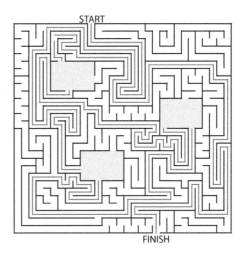

Burrowing owls are small, have no ear tufts, and are active during the day. They have long legs, though, so they can run, which is handy when you spend time on the ground.

VITAL VESSEL

The most important item for travelers on the Oregon Trail was the PRAIRIE SCHOONER.

The Prairie Schooner was smaller and shaped differently than the Conestoga Wagon (a covered wagon) used in the east.

EXTREME OPPOSITES

O	R	E	G	O	N	■	H	A
D	■	T	I	N	Y	■	A	N
D	■	G	I	A	N	T	■	P
R	E	H	I	S	T	O	R	I
C	■	B	E	A	V	E	R	S

The mini beaver, *Microtheriomys brevirhinus*, was squirrel-size and weighed 1–2 pounds. The giant beaver, *Castoroides ohioensis*, was the size of a small black bear, about 6–7 feet long and over 200 pounds.

There was a prehistoric burrowing beaver, too.

1 THING 2 KNOW ABOUT LIGHTHOUSES

 = 2   = 4   = 5

Oregon has 11 lighthouses along the coast.

Two of these 11 lighthouses were privately built but designated *private aids to navigation* by the Coast Guard.

A CLAIM TO FAME

What's a nickname for Hood River?
WINDSURFING CAPITAL OF THE WORLD.

THE ELUSIVE COUGAR

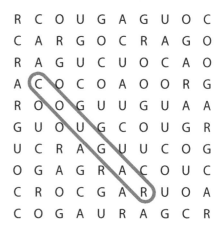

```
R C O U G A G U O C
C A R G O C R A G O
R A G U C U O C A O
A C O C O A O O R G
R O O G U U G U A A
G U O U G C O U G R
U C R A G U U C O G
O G A G R A C O U C
C R O C G A R U O A
C O G A U R A G C R
```

ANIMALS IN TROUBLE

The Pacific Marten, Yellow-billed Cuckoo, Rough popcornflower, Olive ridley sea turtle, and Oregon silverspot butterfly are all endangered or threatened.

The Marshmallow burping frog doesn't exist. Stumpy made it up.

SWITCHAROO 2: A SINKING FEELING

MOUNT MAZAMA - MENT MAZAME - RENT RAZARE - RANT REZARE - RANT RELARE - RACT RELARE - RACT RELAKE - CRAT RELAKE - CRATER LAKE

Mount Mazama was a volcano that blew its top and then caved in over 7,000 years ago. The pit in the caldera filled with water, making Crater Lake, the deepest lake in the U.S., and one of the 10 deepest in the world.

... LIKE A FISH NEEDS A ____

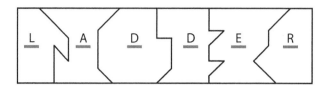

. . . like a fish needs a LADDER.

Fish ladders are no joke. These aren't the kinds of ladders humans use though. Fish ladders are streams that go around dams to let fish swim past the dam to lakes and streams upriver.

Similarly, some dams have locks that allow boats to travel upriver past the dams.

BOOM AND BUST

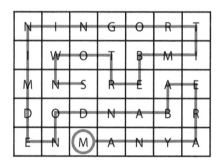

MANY ARE ABANDONED MINING OR TIMBER TOWNS.

WHERE THE FUN IS

Kiteboarding - Hood River

Skiing - Mount Bachelor

Rock climbing - Smith Rock

Surfing - Otter Rock

Rafting - Deschutes River

CARVING THE WAY

Column A		Column B	Extra Letter
NEAR		GROWN	G
POST		RANGE	G
WORN		ALLOW	O
PETS		SPORT	R
WALL		STEEP	E

This throat or neck feature is the Columbia River GORGE.

The Columbia River Gorge is not just a scenic 80-mile drive. It's the only way through the Cascades in this area, which is why there are highways and railroad tracks on both sides of the river.

LIGHTHOUSE IDS

RAIN

GUST

STERN

URGENT

Every lighthouse has a unique flashing pattern called a SIGNATURE.

MAKE IT MYRTLEWOOD

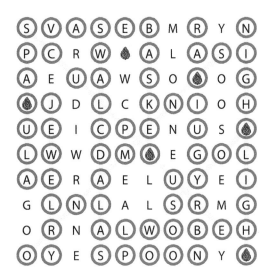

Unused letters: MYRTLEWOOD COINS WERE LEGAL MONEY.

It's true! During the depression in 1933, the town of North Bend used myrtlewood coins because the other kind of money wasn't available. When metal coins were back, people could trade in their myrtle coins, but many kept them as souvenirs.

BACK WORD 2: FAMILY TIES

The western meadowlark is part of the BLACKBIRD family.

A FERNY THING HAPPENED . . .

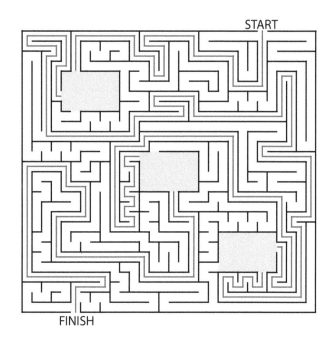

START

FINISH

A young, coiled fern frond is called a "fiddlehead."

MADE IN MARION

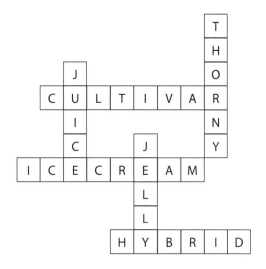

What two blackberry varieties were crossed to make the Marionberry? OLALLIE & CHEHALEM

FOSSIL FINDS

A	L	T	H	O	U	G	H		
S	T	U	D	I	E	D			F
O	R		O	V	E	R			1
0	0		Y	E	A	R	S		
N	E	W		F	O	S	S	I	
L	S		A	R	E		S	T	
I	L	L		F	O	U	N	D	

1 THING 2 KNOW ABOUT GOLD

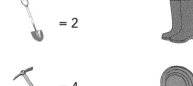

The largest gold nugget found in Oregon weighed 17 pounds.

IN THEIR FOOTSTEPS

What famous people visited Newberry Volcano?
APOLLO ASTRONAUTS TRAINED IN THE CALDERA.

SAND DOLLAR SEARCH

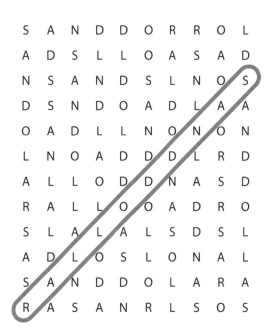

TIDE ZONES: WHO LIVES THERE?

Middle Tide Zone - Purple and ochre sea stars

Spray Zone - Periwinkles and lichens

High Tide Zone - Rock crab and sea lettuce

Low Tide Zone - Red sea urchin and giant green sea anemone

SWITCHAROO 3: RODEO SLOGAN

PENDLETON - LETONPEND - LETOPENND - LETOPEBCD - LETOREBCK - LETEROBCK - LETERBOCK - LETERBUCK - LET 'ER BUCK

A RIVER RUNS THROUGH IT

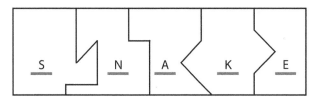

S N A K E

The SNAKE River carved Hells Canyon.

THE GRAY WHALE SCOOP

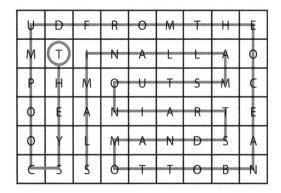

U	D	F	R	O	M	T	H	E
M	T	I	N	A	L	L	A	O
P	H	M	O	U	T	S	M	C
O	E	A	N	I	A	R	T	E
O	Y	L	M	A	N	D	S	A
C	S	S	O	T	T	O	B	N

THEY SCOOP MUD FROM THE OCEAN
BOTTOM AND STRAIN OUT SMALL ANIMALS.

NATIVE OR NOT?

Native: Ringtail, Madrone, Western Snowy
Plover

Invasive: Orange Hawkweed, American Bullfrog,
Nutria

ROCK STAR

Column A	Column B	Extra Letter
NATURE	PIECRUST	S
SEA LION	BASALT	A
BLAST	TOENAILS	T
TIDAL	UNEARTH	H
PICTURE	ROTATE	A
SHORE	DAYLIT	Y
OTTER	PROTECT	C
POTTER	KOSHER	K

Oregon's Rock Star is HAYSTACK Rock.

Haystack Rock is in Cannon Beach. It's 235 feet tall and home to many animals. Tufted puffins and other birds nest on it.

LARGEST FOUND IN THE U.S.—EVER!

TON, MOON, SNOW, WOMAN

TOMANOWOS

Tomanowos is a meteorite discovered in the Willamette Valley. It's sometimes called the Willamette Meteorite, but it was originally named Tomanowos by the Clackamas people.

It's made of iron and nickel and weighs over 15 tons, making it the largest meteorite ever found in the U.S. and the sixth largest in the world. It's on display at the American Museum of Natural History in New York City, but pieces of it have been returned to the

LARGEST FOUND IN THE U.S.—EVER! (CONT.)

Confederated Tribes of Grand Ronde.

Because there was no impact crater where the meteorite was found, scientists believe it landed elsewhere, maybe Canada or Montana, and was brought to the Willamette Valley during glacial floods at the end of the last Ice Age, about 13,000 years ago.

OREGON GROWN

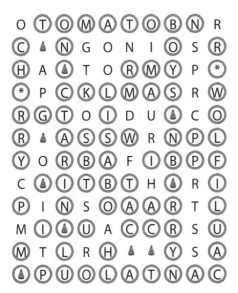

Unused letters: OREGON IS A TOP PRODUCER OF CHRISTMAS TREES.

BACK WORD 3: RABBIT RANGE

Pygmy rabbits live in, eat, and breathe SAGEBRUSH.

ABOUT AN OCTOPUS

START

FINISH

The Giant Pacific Octopus name is no joke. They are the largest octopus species with average adults weighing about 33 pounds with an arm span up to 14 feet. A large adult can be 110 pounds with a 20-foot arm span. Guinness World Records lists the largest at 300 pounds with a 32-foot arm span. Let's just say they're giant, okay?

Giant Pacific Octopuses don't have fur, but they have special pigment cells in their skin that allow them to change color and texture to blend with their environment.

MULTNOMAH FALLS

Multnomah Falls is a PERENNIAL WATERFALL.

Big word alert! *Perennial* means it flows year-round. It can do this because in addition to rainfall and snowmelt, the falls are fed by a spring.

MOVE OVER, BLUE WHALE

What has disturbed the blue whale's place in the world?

A		H	O	N	E	Y		M
U	S	H	R	O	O	M		T
H	A	T		I	S		T	H
E		L	A	R	G	E	S	T
	O	R	G	A	N	I	S	M
	O	N		E	A	R	T	H

A mushroom is more than the stem and cap we see above ground. Below ground, mushrooms might be connected, making one giant organism. The one here in Oregon covers almost 4 square miles. That's about 1,665 football fields!

A blue whale is still the largest *animal* on Earth though.

1 THING 2 KNOW ABOUT WEIRD PORTLAND

 = 6   = 8   = 10

The World's Smallest Park in Portland, Oregon, is 24 inches in diameter.

Mill Ends Park, located in a median strip on SW Naito Parkway in Portland was officially designated a city park and "the only leprechaun colony west of Ireland" on March 17, 1976, St. Patrick's Day. The town of Talent, Oregon, aims to unseat the current Smallest Park with an even tinier, bee-friendly park.

PEST CONTROL

A BAT CAN EAT A THOUSAND INSECTS IN AN HOUR.

ROCKHOUND

```
T R T H U N D E R T U T
G H H U G G E R H U H G
T H U N D E R E G N U E
G D N N U H E U N N G G
E N D T G D T D G D G R
R G E G N E R D E E E E
E U R U T G R N R R R D
D(T H U N D E R E G G)N
N T E D N U H T D G U U
U G G T G E R E N E G H
H E D G E R E D N U H T
T H U N D E R R E G G U
```

MASCOT LOVE

Timber Joey - MLS Soccer

Benny Beaver - Oregon State University

The Duck - University of Oregon

Dillon T. Pickle - Portland Collegiate Summer Baseball League

SWITCHAROO 4: PLANT A PEAR TREE

ROOTSTOCK - RATSTCK - RATFGCK - TFARGCK - GRAFT - GRANT - GRIONT - GSCIONT - SCION

Very clever, Queenie! Okay, friends, I hope you chipped away at that as I did.

Weird word alert! A scion (say SI-uhn) is a twig or bud cut from one tree so that it can be grafted (attached) onto the root of another tree. The two parts grow together and produce a tree.

People do this for lots of reasons. For instance, the scion of a tasty pear tree might be grafted onto the rootstock of a disease-resistant, short tree so that the pears are disease-free and easier to pick.

ON THE NOSE

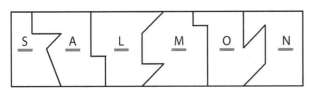

This hooked nose animal is the SALMON.

When male salmon enter fresh water to spawn, their noses change shape.

COLOR ME CURIOUS

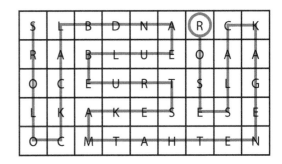

ROSES LACK A GENE THAT MAKES TRUE-BLUE AND BLACK COLORS.

If you see a blue rose, you know it has been genetically modified or dyed.

THE LAY OF THE LANDMARKS

Attilio Pusterla's Column - Astoria

Vista House - Columbia River Gorge

International Rose Test Garden - Portland

Cheese Factory - Tillamook

Spruce Goose - McMinnville

The Attilio Pusterla Column is really called the Astoria Column, but that kinda gives the answer away.

The Spruce Goose is the largest wooden airplane ever built.

BEACH TREASURES

Column A	Column B	Extra Letter
MARGINS	PROCESS	S
SECRET	PETRIFY	F
BURIED	RECITES	I
CORPSE	ORGANISM	O
REACH	REBUILD	L
PYRITE	SEMINARS	S
REMAINS	SEARCH	S

You might find these on Oregon's beaches: FOSSILS.

STATE SYMBOLS

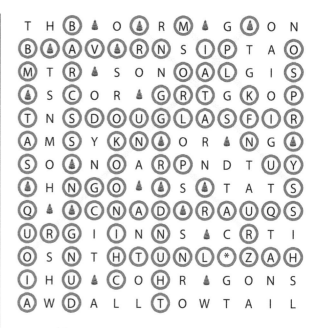

Unused letters: THE OREGON STATE SONG IS "OREGON, MY OREGON," AND THE STATE INSECT IS THE OREGON SWALLOWTAIL.

NATURE'S BONSAI

SEEK, ZERO, STORM, HUMOR, SHORE, RUSTLE

KRUMMHOLZ TREES

Big word alert! Say krum-hōltz.

Look on the cliffs at the coast for misshapen trees. You can tell the direction the wind mostly blows by the way the trees are growing.

BACK WORD 4: A BURROWER?

There's plenty to explore in Oregon if you're a SPELEOLOGIST.

Big word alert! A speleologist is someone who studies caves. Maybe you've heard the word "spelunking," which is the act of exploring caves. To go spelunking is to go caving.

FRUIT LOOP

START FINISH

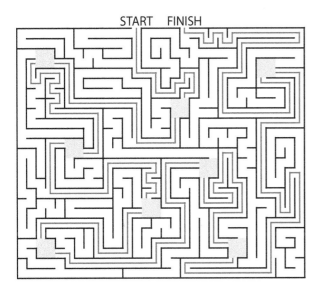

HiDDEN iN PLAiN SiGHT

```
E               M               P
C               Y               A
O               S               R
L    N O C T U R N A L
O               E               C
G L I D E R     H
Y               Y               U
                                T
        S E C R E T
```

Humboldt's Flying Squirrels are a CRYPTIC
SPECIES.

CERTIFICATE OF MEMBERSHIP

This certifies that

_____

(print your name here)

has completed the rigorous, head-scratching, mind-boggling, brain-building challenges in

THE PUZZLER'S GUIDE TO OREGON

and has demonstrated extraordinary stick-to-it-iveness,
thereby earning membership in the official

PUZZLER'S CLUB

 CHIPPER

 QUEENIE

 SPOT

 STUMPY

Printed in the USA
CPSIA information can be obtained
at www.ICGtesting.com
JSHW042029031023
49602JS00006B/6